Windows and Doors

A Book of Poetry

RICHARD ROBINSON

Sunny Lou Publishing Company
Portland, Oregon, USA
http://www.sunnyloupublishing.com

Corrected: 2024 April 26
Original Publication Date: 2024 Mar 8

ISBN: 978-1-955392-61-7

Contents

Windows
and Doors

2024

New Archangel

When I walked onto that terrace,
I realized that I was the pariah;
In any other worldly place,
I would tell you I am the messiah.

But at home my case is no better,
Xanthippe is the eternal shrew;
Suggesting for holidays Dutch Harbor,
I am berated like a loon.

I get no love in Portland, Oregon,
Drifts my way no charity or kindnesse;
Like a shipwrack on the horizon,
I am lonely from vespers to nones.

Now I long to be north of Wrangell,
Where the glaciers crack and roar,
Or beside the bay of New Archangel,
Spearing salmon, out of doors.

The Wind Does Blow

The wind does blow, the breeze does sough,
The wrennes do twitter in the barren bough,
And in the thorns and amongst the reeds,
The tears do flow, the heart does bleed. –

And I am leaving now: I will not be here tomorrow.

The rain does fall, the ground does glisten,
The briddes and bestes do quiet now and listen;
Whenas before they did leap and amble,
Today they tarry in the barren bramble, –

And hark, ye Angels! Hark ye, good Christians!

Holy Rood

Lord, you know I need a drink,
Too many things I'm working on –
I have not got the time to think
And even less to write a poem.

I will find me a bar where brood
The Scotch or the Irish or English,
And sing a song of Holy Rood,
And Christ Jesus, damn it!

Heaven and Skies

In my heart of hearts,
there is a place, a part,
a cubbyhole for two,
for me and for you.

In my eye of eyes
are heaven and skies
where two creatures sing
and pass by on wing.

If ever in this heart
there were a place, a part
where lovers could meet,
and not find defeat

For the better part
Of one hour, my heart
Might be whole again
And my eyes wide open.

Larch Mountain

The easterly blew with frozen blasts;
The tall trees bent like mizzenmasts.

The Easterly

Up there, the tall and stately fir trees
Standing against the sky were couth,
The trunks barely bent in the breeze;

But the branches swept the blowy lift
Like, with broomy stumps, the youth
In a description of morning by Swift.

In Even and Sorrow

The sky was grey-pinking, the rain had stopped,
It was a beautifully melancholic morning,
I was deliciously alone in my room, enjoying
The silence; the sun rose and made me start;

Gay was my heart, and fearless was my soul;
Afternoon came and I worked in the yard
Picking up branches, many thick and hard,
That a frozen rain and furious wind felled

In the storm. Late afternoon, I was restless;
I did not feel so invincible now, did I ever?
The morning was promising, but the hour
Of darkness was on me, and I felt powerless.

What man will rise elated to God on the morrow
Only to suffer in his soul in even and sorrow?

Pathetic

I am so utterly alone, and pathetic,
My heart bleeds like St. Teresa's
In Richard Crashaw's poem;

Of friends I have none, save you,
O my Lady, and a questioning heart
That prizes you and fears you.

My enemies are multiple and fleet,
They do not come to the temple
And worship at her conquering feet.

My wife and son, my mother
And brothers, all friends and lovers –
Are all so furiously against her...

I am so utterly alone, and pathetic,
My heart bleeds like St. Teresa's
In Richard Crashaw's poem.

2023

A Sentimental Walk

Moi j'errais tout seul, promenant ma plaie. –
"Promenade Sentimentale," *Poèmes saturniens,* PAUL
VERLAINE

Had the setting sun fired its last rays?
Maybe not. It was time for a sandwich.
The wind cradled some wan nenuphars?
Possibly, but I could not tell you which.

I erred alone, it is true, walking my wound
Along the channel just north of the hotel,
And headed toward Kapahulu, led on
By the bare buttocks of a surfer girl

Who unabashedly appeared out of nowhere
Reminding me of no one. No teals called out
Each to each, no northern cardinals' wings beat,
No mermaids sang, no fins splashed water...

I walked my wound and did not die that day.
A younger version of myself might have, –
Longing, lonely, solicitous, desperate.
Older now, jaded, I buttoned my sleeves.

Lo Ferm Voler Qu'el Cor M'intra[1]

The firm desire that **enters** my heart
Cannot be driven out by the beak or **nail**
Of slanderers, who by backbiting harm **souls**;
And since I dare not beat him with switch or **rod**,
I will find my joy, there where there are no **uncles**,
Secretly in gardens or inside a **chamber**.

When I think of her **chamber**
Where, to my detriment, I know no man **enters**, –
Indeed, it is the same for brothers or **uncles** –
I tremble all over, even to my **nails**,
Just like a child before the **rod**:
So afraid am I lest I be far away from her **soul**.

If I were there in body, but not **soul**,
And she consented to hide me in her **chamber**,
Which hurts me more than blows of the **rod**
Thinking on it, there where her servant **enters** not:
I will be with her the entire time like flesh to **nails**
And will disregard the counsel of friends or **uncles**.

Indeed, not even my **uncle's** sister
Have I loved so much as I love her, by my **soul**!
She who is closer to me than fingers to **nails**,
If it pleased her, I would gladly be in her **chamber**:

[1]Englished from the Occitan poem of the same name, written by *il miglior fabbro*, Arnaut Daniel.

Making love to her as desire **enters**
My heart, stronger than a man with a feeble **rod**.

Since the time that dry **rods** flowered
And Adam begat nephews and **uncles**,
Such fine love as what **enters** my heart
Is unlike any has entered another man's heart or **soul**;
Wherever she is, in piazza or in **chamber**,
My heart is near her like a **nail** to the finger.

Thus does it happen that my heart, like **nails**,
Clings to her like the outer bark to a **rod**;
For she is my joy in both palace and **chamber**,
And I love her more than my brothers, parents, or
      uncles.
I trust that in paradise my **soul**'s joy will be double
If ever a man who loves her **enters** there.

Arnaut sends this song of **nail** and **uncle**,
To please her who possesses his **rod**'s **soul,**
His *Desire*, which is worthy to **enter** her **chamber**.

Everything is January

A crack in the sky, snowberries, and a pale yellow aster
– "A Crack in the Sky; On a Path, a Winter Flower,"
Ourigan, Oregon, ANONYMOUS

Everything is January for me.
Winter, the darling month of lovers,
Is a time of betrayal and alchemy;
It is the plot of April and November,
Or Oceanus and Tethys of Maeander.
It is, as you know, a pocketful of snowberries, –
Sometimes, do you revisit our memories?

Everything is the Epiphany for me.
A Cana wedding for good Christians,
It is the water, wine, and three Marys
Who anoint our feet with best intentions.
It is Lot with his daughters' pretensions.
Life, believe me, is a pocketful of snowberries, –
Sometimes, do you revisit our memories?

In the Air

The fresh smell of winter forest,
the ground covered in snow,
but the perception much higher than that,
lofty, hovering, in the air,
above the windows, above the eaves.
The fresh smell of snow in the air;

But that's not it.

Sleeping, you missed the morning light,
you missed the faint yellow and blue line
that heralds morning,
the trembling stillness in the air,
you missed the liveliness of nature.
You missed Aurora, rising, in the air.

But that's not it.

Warm within (but not so warm within)
from behind the frosted window
I could smell the snow
on the ground, in the air,
I could smell the snow for the trees.
There were premonitions in the air.

But that's not it.

Caged

What kind of man is that, who would be caged,
Like a common budgie, cockatiel, or parrot,
As you see me, you think: I do allow it,
And acting so, you would know my rage.

Did you think I was a man who could be caged?

Is This Your Love

Nine Moneths I liu'd – 'Tis a Pity, JOHN FORD

All my burnt bridges, all my sunken boats,
All the damage I've done to her and most, –
Is this your loue Grimaldi? Fie, t'is naught.

Sweet faint failure; ripe and randy regret,
Hymen's broken vows on softer carpet, –
Welcome sweete night, the Euening crownes the day.

I loved your heart; whate'er with that was wrong?
Your tender temple, and glances sidelong –
For nine Moneths space, in secret I enjoy'd

Your matchless beauty, and your gay attires, –
Of one so young, so rich in nature's store,
Who could not say, 'Tis pitty shee's a Whore?

Odio e Amo

How can I love, when all I have is hate;
People are shallow, cold, stupid, selfish,
Judgmental, hypocritical, and vain;
They pull the wool down over others' eyes.

But supposing I am no better than they,
Why should I seek out their company then,
I have my own foul self to consort with:
I'm not so much the comedian of late.

In the future, in a forgotten corner
Of a forsaken place, amidst the debris,
Some sorry sack reader, hoping to escape
Life in a book I happened to scrape together,
Might read what I have written and say:
"I like this fellow: we are the same."

Poor in Spirit

September was still, the morning air was cool;
A message from snow-capped Mt. Hood said:
"Break your long rest, lazy bones, sleepy head;
Get out of bed, put on the fire more fuel."

So I did; and my wife added a blanket
To our bed, such as it is, – foam mattress
On the ground: we live these days in such distress,
Remembering when life was a banquet.

I'm not so old as to forget the sweetness
Of days when a bottle of Rhine wine, cheese,
And bread made a complete meal that pleased us;
In our poverty was a joy in simpleness.

Our love of simpleness has left us long since,
Now we are poor in both spirit and finance.

Night Falls Furiously

Pierrot, qui n'a rien d'un Clitandre,
vide un flacon sans plus attendre,
– *"Pantomine," Fêtes galantes,* PAUL VERLAINE

Night falls furiously like the hangman
Pulling a burlap bag over the blond head of
Another dying day for the American.

And here come the bone-and-rag men!...
Sorting through garbage cans on the street
With the dexterity of rice pickers from Xiamen.

Individual freedom is prized over all else
In a routing republic that once prided itself
On a narrow-waisted Protestant work ethic.

Henry David meanwhile castrates himself,
Sows pond sewage into the scabrous mouth of
The first doting demoiselle he comes across.

"Pass it along," he says, smiling.
"Who, what?" Levidulcia canters. "The wife, the
　　　clap."
And Charlemont restores dignity to the tragedy.

In this way, the *invraisemblables* become intimates.
And looking back over a creaking gunwale,
Loomis vanishes into the white-capped waves.

Costermongers and louche baristas wear

All the colors of a garish rainbow on their
Recycled-plastic sleeves, like fasces.

Ingenuously they think love wins;
But the iron boot will crush them like grass blades
And the New World will be light and sweetness
          again.

The Charity of Dolores

*Though I speak with the tongues of men and of angels,
and have not charity, I am become as sounding brass,
or a tinkling cymbal.* 1 Corinthians 13:1, KJV

September was cool, after the August heat
Broke in Pendleton; later we languished
Around the swimming pool, at a Super 8,
Sipping margaritas or chocolate milk.

In the calico dress you wore, not large
But *grande,* you played solitaire til dusk;
Sometimes, leaning over your marked cards,
You let me see everything in your hand.

> *Do you love me?*
> *Like a child loves its mother.*
> *Do you love me?*
> *Like a bird the sky.*

In Yakima we stopped for a late lunch;
Rode through the historic downtown and saw
A bare-chested Indian man hopped up
On sunshine, pushing a shopping cart.

Semblance of a boudoir in a cheap motel,–
Psyche and Eros, and all that entailed:
We knew each other, you cried, *et al.,*
And I looked out the window, darkly.

> *Will you love me at nine?*

I will love you like the night.
Will you love me at nine?
I will love you, now good night.

Armenian Blackberry

O *Rubus armeniacus*, you fell
From the sky, or a seed or a drupe did,
From a bird's beak or bum, – who could tell?
That in my neighbor's Hawthorne tree was hid
The sower of an invasive species;
You fell, and now you dominate the garden
With tart berries that grew out of feces, –
Juicy in June, in September they harden –

Old Love! our story of strange similarity,
Our romance no less serendipitous,
Meets by chance with tacit terribility, –
Do you think our hearts were precipitous?
We loved each other once, and will again,
When geese return and the dark days lengthen.

The White Walnut

Autumn is icumen in, and the leaflets
Of the White Walnut are falling, green,
Yellow and green, while the leafstalks set
Against the sky scratch it, aquamarine.

Juglans cinerea has a thick green crown
In summer, but is deciduous and drops
Its leafstalks, everichon, to the ground
By October or November, and stops.

I look out my window and I wonder
How many seasons it has, this old tree,
Before it gives up the soul, and whether
Its saplings will recall it when it leafs.
The sap runs cold in the heart of winter,
The fire dies, shoots from the trunk splinter.

Belladonna

You are the belladonna, with leaves oblate,
Margins entire, and tips acuminate;
I love your easy elegance, mauve, jade;
On every other plant you cast a shade.

You are the Lady Atropos, your eyes
Are deep black pools, ever widening skies;
I'm intoxicated just looking on you.
You are Sola, Sinead, Cleo, Salo.

It was Fate that dropped you in my garden:
You are death, and the Inexorable One.
The little bird that brought you here: Lachesis,
Necessity, the Holy Mother of Jesus.

A summer breeze blows on my nape, neck;
What hazard will your fortune bring me, wreck?

Wizened Apples

Thinke not cause men flatt'ring say,
Y' are fresh as Aprill, sweet as May...
– "To A. L.: Perswasions to loue." Thomas Carew

The better half of a woman's beauty
Shines in the effulgency of her youth;
With age come the side-effects of gravity,
In time she exchanges beauty for truth.

But men, some grow wiser not less;
They show honesty in lines of their face;
Their appeal comes from being dauntless;
Of any fear of death they have no trace.

Who covets your wizened apples now, Blanche?
Fruit maggots worm through their exocarp;
When ripened peaches fall from the branch,
What Tom or Dick will relish their endocarp?

Half a man and half a woman make one;
The rest rots in the dirt and rain and sun.

Maint Clouds in God's Heaven

At the end of the Oregon Trail

In the road, in the garbage, in the gutter,
Is a discarded hypodermic needle;
A broken-down car with a smashed windshield;
Bicycle tires, frames, chains, a gas burner,
A tent on the sidewalk, or three or four;
And, wearing a surgical mask, waving,
Pupils dilated from methamphetamine,
A ruined man begs in the street divider.

Above all this, maint clouds in God's heaven,
Like sea nymphs bathing in glorious light,
A sky, azure on gold, gules on white,
Over the most majestic range of mountain
E'er seen on earth; – an even so quiet
Both bird and beast were straining to hear it.

The Pendleton Rodeo

The Pendleton rodeo is a fine occasion
To be around people close to the dirt,
Sitting on the bleachers, squirting their squirt,
Yelling, hollering, cheering on the men
And women riding in competition.
I love to watch them roughstock or polebend,
I love to drink a cold beer to them and,
Cheering them on, shout out loud: "Hold on!"

But considering this, after a moment,
And putting the rodeo in context,
I feel that I have had my entertainment
For the day, and this event is pretext
For not grappling with the presentiment
That life escapes me, and death is next.

Michael!

> *Your pretty tale beguiles the weary way.* – Arden of
> Faversham

You will have no redemption, Michael!
Desirous of Susan, Alice's saucy maid.
You are lost in a poplar coppice or glade;
And you will find yourself alone withal,

By yourself, with yourself, and no escape.
People everywhere, and not a friend to lean on:
You choose: badlands or the Septentrion,
Or the Antartica, south of the Cape.

All hope is drowned, you mistook God's direction,
And like the Ancient Mariner you abide,
Scanning the searing sea for a telling tide,
While Life in Death stifles everich redress.

Your industry alone will bring no release;
Your life wavers, and from bad to worse proceeds.

Tenino

Disturbed thoughts drives me from company – Arden of
Faversham

Today I walked the dog along the cliff,
Fine coistrel that I am, near like a queynte;
As you know me, you know well my complaint:
Ships don't sail to port that sail for Cardiff.

But on murd'rous highways, south of Olympia,
In a sweltering sun, I saw more ghosts
And dark thoughts crowd about me in hosts
Than allotropes in black or yellow arsenic, –

More ghosts than Centralia's shade was cool,
Or Northwest ales are quenching to the thirst;
It will not be the last time a man, or first,
Sought respite in God's good swimming pool.

But Life in Death grabbed my wavering wrists
And steered the ship from running adrift.

No One Dared to Ask

Before the night fell, a breeze pulled on the sky
And the air stirred in the trees; a golden tabby
Stalked slowly along the base of the fence,
And held its breath in the deteriorating ivy.

Before the night fell, a lazy breeze
Painted itself in the atmosphere and died,
And in the branches, and on the leaves,
A question hovered that no one dared to ask.

The Dalles

I will be leaving soon, my time and presence
Are limited, nearly exhausted. Incorporeal,
Other than electronic receipts, no durable evidence
Will remain that I passed through The Dalles.

This page, then, is the vestige, the artefact
That I was here. You won't find me in the water,
In the sky, or in the cormorants, double-crested:
Deflected are my sounds; my ripples ring farther.

You won't find me in the bunch grass, or the stalks
Of quamash in front yards, or the sweetgum
Leaves on Court St., or around Pulpit Rock.

You will not see me, or know if I was glum,
Joyful, anxious, calm, with or without a face.
You will not hear me; I leave not a trace.

The U.S. Post Office Building

The simple elegance of your shape,
Your smooth, composite columns;
The sober sandstone of your face,
At the corner of 2nd St. and Union.

The stillness of a summer evening,
Ruptured only by the comment
Of a tangle of local Towhee,
Made for a mystical moment –

All that was good, right, round;
But Tenino sandstone like Amerindians
Displaced by cement and Europeans –

Did it need to go? And the silence
Broken by the highway sounds –
How is that not grievous violence?

Buntings

The birds are calling, each to each,
On branches, behind leaves;
They call amidst the foliage,
With love in their bosoms and beaks.

The sun, yellow, rises in the east;
It illuminates the horizons,
Shines on the grasses, on the peaks,
Brings warmth, stirs passions.

But who calls to me, at this hour?
With my heart gript by rime,
Who calls to the sunburnt scyther,

The dusty winnower in a ruined tower,[2]
Who calls to the man out of time?
Ah, is that you, Morning Star?

---

[2]*Je suis le ténébreux, le veuf, l'inconsolé,/ Le prince d'Aquitaine à la tour abolie* – "El Desdichado," *Les Chimères,* Gérard de Nerval.

Brown Headed Cowbird

Brown headed cowbird,
May I ask you a favor – one day,
You must give me your word, –
Tell me what you say;

I saw you and your companion,
Similar in beak to a bunting, –
A lithesome golden specimen, –
Flittering, twittering,

On the branches... – O, my oath!
Pray do not tell my wife, –
I saw you. In all my life,

How I admired you both,
Singing each to each in song, –
"Who, us? You have it wrong."

Storm Clouds

I wish I could say, our love will last forever,
But will it last one more day even? In eternity,
One day is a long time. Storm clouds gather
On the horizon and reindeer nibble on chicory.

I wished I could say our love will last an eternity –
But will it, after such tempestuous weather?
Is our love dead then, after five and twenty –
In such cold, will the quamash last to December?

Loophole II

How to tell X*** that our life together was spent?
Due decennia and counting is not exactly two cents.
I would not give it up. You would not give it up?
You are a pretty face, but that is not enough.

Of all the beautiful places we visited together:
Memaloose State Park, Indian graveyards –
No people! Golden beaches measuring for miles;
Lighthouses, sunken cities, ancient glyphs on igneous
        rock piles.

What did you think I wanted to do, – look and chat?
How to convey to you the boredom I am at.
You are a knot of commonplace thought and stance.
Was it not third grade when I mastered this round
        dance?

I showed you beaches where two or one
Could swim, play: I tried to be the good cousin.
But your vessel hummed at me beneath the table.
Something nagged at me beneath your blouse, under
        the maples.

That I would invite you, – did you expect it? –
On long vistas of the Columbia River Gorge at sunset,
Or to walk for an eternity holding hands,
Only to make memories to tell our grandparents?

I have farrow fields to plow, autumn seeds to cast.

Am I a breath of fresh air, or a knot of poisonous gas?
Am I Eros, Swedenborg, Restif de la Bretonne, or
      Byron?
Look out your arrowslit, my sweet, and ponder.

Another Day of Darkness

The Bridegroom's doors are opened wide – "The Rime
of the Ancient Mariner," *The Lyrical Ballads*, SAMUEL
TAYLOR COLERIDGE

Another day of darkness, another day of drear
In the jaundiced Western hemisphere;
Stuck behind moral lapses and the door,
Looking out windows, drowning in the pour, –
My life founders in separateness and death.
My feet are cold, and fetid is my breath.

Ghost of the past inspiriting me, sprite
Of rainy days and nights, – archangel of light!
Bad advocate who visits me as I flounder,
Soul of demons, and the Weird ponderer
Of indiscretions and inscrutable ways, –
O leave me now, long and lonely days!

My hate is higher than the Douglas fir trees,
My rancor broader than the Columbia,
My bile bitterer than the nightshade,
My blood colder than the snowcapped Cascades, –
In a temperate spring or torrid summer,
Who dares greet the unbearable bearer?

Naked Beauty

You abhorred a naked beauty, –
It is hard to stomach and alarming;
You preferred a sort of insincerity
And cruelty; it made you feel charming.

I showed you candidness, generosity,
A human heart in brutal climates,
You served me *hong dou*, they made me fart;
I nearly cried, "such malfaisance."

And They Do Wound Me

Mes pleurs sont à moi, nul au monde
Ne les a comptés ni reçues;
Pas un œil étranger qui sonde
Les désespoirs que j'ai conçus.
– "Adieux a la Poésie," L. ACKERMANN

And they do wound me with deep despyte,
From morning to noon, evening to midnight,
Family, colleagues, neighbors, friends,
Some for no reason, others with hidden ends.

They do slay, gag, disembowel, wound, –
My feet are like a hare's chased by a hound.
Not appreciating other beautiful look
Than what is on the Internet or Facebook,

They say treacherous things behind my back,
Defensive now, they then go on the attack, –
There is no respite for a naïve, naked soul
Who, head long in the clouds, falls into a hole.

Pang

The song, the dream, the tape's slowdown,
A bell, the back-pedaling guitar,
And Mei Pang whispering: "John."

What is there not to adore? Afar
I find your face a silver-lined moon,
And your lips, upcurled, are

Something to covet, to ponder on.
I find your story of the "weekend"
Like several stanzas out of Byron:

Don Juan, or *Childe Harold*;
That man's fragile myth, your sexuality.
What's there not to like at all?

L'Hôtel Clarendon

Your lack of joy, our lack of enthusiasms,
Under coffered ceilings, beneath copper roofs;
On our second honeymoon, a lack of org*sms
Was something to be noted and reproved.

I cannot make you love me, in any way but one;
Over the St. Lawrence River today shines the sun
Nine ways to Wednesday, and then some;
Did we come to Québec City only to eat salmon?

In the dark of night, when the Anglican steeple
Pricks the sky, and the Acadian people
Let down their hair, and lift up their glasses,
Some people touch some people's *sses...

Your lack of joy, our lack of enthusiasms,
Under coffered ceilings, beneath copper roofs.

La Place D'Youville

I held your hand, we walked through the snow,
In my heart was something you did not know;
On the plains of Abraham, a sadness gripped me:
A coldness in the ground, in the roots of a tree –

The oak trees beside the National Assembly
Which held on to their leaves, or four or three,
Whilst Mlle. de la Vallée, forty years earlier,
Between two shifts, with nothing to show for her... –

By the Porte St. Jean, at the Place D'Youville,
We strapped on our blades and took several laps...
I tripped, you laughed, but picked myself back up;
Back to the hotel, we later climbed the hill.

I held your hand, we walked through the snow,
In my heart was something you did not know.

Fair Was Your Skin

Fair was your skin, no whiter than skimmed *dofu;*
Big were your eyes, but no bigger than the moon;
Your teeth were pearls, I counted them: two and
      thirty,
Your breasts, small, I saw them: they were alert;

The sound of your voice was melodic, sweet;
The pitch like that of finches, high, singing,
Like the girl on the playground that one meets
As a child, the both of us – when we were green.

The hills where we played were dark and low,
Thick and heavy was the smell of the sage;
Infused was the evening with a coppery glow,
When we watched the horizon as teenagers.

You did not give me more than I asked for,
I gave you no more than my word.

May in December

I came here today to be with you; knowing
You are far, infinitely far from me,
Surrounded by the tables and wainscoting
That once wrapped us like a dirty bedsheet.

Was it a felony for us to meet?
We met privately, in a public place, –
Your comely youth and lust for life, my big feet.
After two Scottish ales, and sitting face

To face with you in silent conversation,
Can you fault me wanting to drown the ghost?
For *sept ans, deux mois*, you were my obsession.
I believed you believed me to be honest...

Now you are gone away, – was it a dream,
A sexagenarian's love, or something baser?
Today, it feels more like a hangover than
The headiness of May in December.

Down

The table is turning, the walls are breathing,
The ground beneath my feet is giving.
And I'm drowning, going down, down,
The roof is rising, the clouds are turning brown.

And then, spack! – things crumble and break;
I lie in frozen catalepsy in a lake,
More at the middle than at the edges
Family members, friends, are behind hedges.

The air is cold through open windows,
Smelling of Switzerland and the snow,
Like footprints in the mud, – all my misdeeds,
All my irreligious behaviors, lead

Me to escape life, to find some retreat,
Alone in a place with no human teat
To latch on to, to comfort, to console me,
Beneath dark waters, tangled in algae.

New Ephemera

What are the roots that clutch, what the tendril
That digs into a rock and holds on to it.
Death is fond, but no sooner does the thrill
Stop than sunlight, on dull leaf edges, glints.

The sun behind the ridge in early morning,
The ubiquitous crow cawing in the sky,
Out of sight, and me flatfooted standing
In the valley, undone, and wishing to cry.

For people are hypocritical, and love,
Though rich, has egos that are in contest
With words emerging from a glossy mouth.
The time for patience is not just in the past.
No sooner does night's terror lighten, lift,
Than new ephemera stir and softly shift.

The Snow Is Melting

The snow is melting, fast it shall be gone;
My heart, heavy, can breathe again and soon
I see through the windows of my room
Empty patches on the branches and lawn.

The sun shines, dissolves the leftover snow,
Like a judge the sentence, granting reprieve;
New feelings will lighten the heart now; love
Will naturally lift what was brought so low.

Loophole I

I don't want to be here.
The juncos are too noisy,
dark-eyed, scratching
the ground with a fever.

And the American robins,
red-breasted *everichon*,
fighting without reasons –
they see their reflection

in the glass, no?
I don't want to be here,
looking out a loophole
at hawthorn and cedar.

2022

Common Rush

Of all the things that fell into my yard,
Droppings, debris, rubber bands, and what all,
By æroplanes passing over head, or bird,
Or by act of God, *damnum fatale.*

Tips of branches that fell and fell again
Whence and wherefore nobody could guess,
It was not the rain, it was not the wind,
But the Paraclete that visited us...[3]

Seeds of a capsule of the common rush,
Naturally sown, now tall twelve inches
After twenty months, the *Juncus effusus,*
A forage for mice, a shelter for finches.

O *Juncus effusus,* you make me glad
Whenever I see you and my heart was sad.

---

[3]*si enim non abiero, Paraclitus non veniet ad vos; si autem abiero, mittam eum ad vos*: John 16:7, Vulgate.

Fluid

And the wind blew in the trees,
and the trees blew in the wind,
and everything was fluid: peace,
love, time, religion, space, –
everything, but understanding.

There Will be Time

In all the world, there will be time,
To seed the fragrant hyacinths,
In a fertile ground behind the fence
Overrun by wild amaranths –

Seeded by the wind, dropped by angels
Maybe, or deposited by a silly wren,
And which the gardener does not weed,
Considering them venerated.

In all the world, there will be time,
To call each other out, sisters
And mothers, enemies and neighbors,
Putting on our yellow kid gloves.

In all the world, in all the world –
I remember I gave you a dress once:
You never put it on. You blushed
Red like the blood of empresses

That Chinese history is filled with.
I remember how you sacrificed your sleep once
When I went to work early,
To keep our young love fresh.

ENVOI

We were young, we loved each other –

We love each other still; – but did not speak much
      then
Lest instinctively a word spoken
In anger or out of selfishness or regret
Be not forgiven or forgotten so easily.

There will be time, in all the world...
To harvest the past, and to fully appreciate
The life we lived together, the moments we had,
When, now, the one thing we do have is time.
We were so very hurried then.

My Muse Went Missing

My muse went missing, I went to find her;
Where, o where have you gone, my little dar':
I found shooting stars, incarnadine columbines,
In riparian meadows below the timberline.

> *I have gone to gather the morning dew*
> *Before the heat of a summer day,*
> *Before they wither and die on a season,*
> *Before the skies turn cold and gray.*

My muse went missing, I went to find her;
O where have you gone, my stone breaker:
From Elk Mountain, I grimped up Gorge Ridge trail,
I found purple lupine in subalpine vales.

> *I have gone to inhale the evening air*
> *Before the cold of night sets in,*
> *Before the good God calls me,*
> *Before stiffness fills my limbs.*

My muse went missing, I went to find her;
Where have you gone, my little white flower:
I hunted frantically in the scree and talus, –
No love or kindness, I found only malice.

ENVOI

My heart withers on the vine –

In all the world, on all the mountain,
    Where is there more bitter wine,
Or a drier source or fountain,
    After losing the loved one,
Being without family or friend.

Anti-Fascist

"Someone said you're 'anti-fascist,' in a dream" –
I didn't even know what that means; –
A sign displayed in a shop window, a hand...
You meant it as a slur, a reprimand.

I stood behind you, my head on your shoulder,
In my hand, your breast; I grew bolder.
"I'm dreaming," I said: in life you're not so gentle.
My inability to see your face was instrumental.

You quoted a man, dictating how I should act;
Someone on the Internet, his words, fact.
How to conform to the monetized videos
You watch; there is a cost to such *prodeos*.

And you who were, for many years, my tender wife,
Are now the cause of the greater part of our strife.

The Vision Passed

The wrens, hidden in nature, called each to each,
The morning sun rose in the east, pink, peach;
Never had I seen a sunrise light the sky,
In spring, in youth, so magnificently.

I was on a verdant hill, looking out;
In my mind and heart, no room for doubt:
I stood on the verge of an earthly Paradise,
And the vision passed before my eyes.

From Quilcene to Sequim

Through an old-growth forest –
Hemlock, cedar, maple, spruce, –
And the young undergrowth of trees:
Old sword fern, Oregon grape,
And the leathery-leaf Salal
With its dangling, translucent-white globules,
And the promise of blue berries,
Blue in summer, blue against the sky,
By a road where future venison
Stood standing, waiting to cross,
And pre-Columbian Indians, invisible
To the naked eye, made no sign.

By the highway, brutal sometimes,
From Quilcene to Sequim,
Foxglove spears, mauve, crimson,
Nature's banners, pennants, or lances;
Daisies, always new and gleeful,
Meadows of them, white, yellow
Their perpetually smiling faces,
Full of the promises of youth,
With the inevitability of the ages,
Which weighs down on the leaves
With the dew of the sea and the eventual return
Of anadromous salmon
To the pools they came from.

The Earnestness of an Afternoon

O grands doux frênes qui souriez,
Nulle âme au bois — dès mainte année —
– "At Helen's Grave", *Swans*, FRANCIS VIELÉ-GRIFFIN

Of an afternoon,
Late, on a Thursday, in early June,
Before a faint monsoon

An old man, whose passion is risible
An old man whose passion is as serious as a grebe
A lone grebe paddling frantically at the surface of a
        water
In concentric circles

And a young man whose seriousness is risible;
A young man's seriousness risible as the rain
And the menace of meteorology laughing with
        disdain
It is risible like our separation
It is risible like the pain

The yellow stubble of low lying hills in East Oregon
And the river that passes through them like a vein
Is nothing compared to the lush valleys of West
        Oregon
Where the verdure of old rain forests causes pain

An overcast sky recomforts

A disturbed sky like an overturned field infuses
            thoughts of relief
A cathartic buildup of the elements, and the muted
            pressure of rain
The muted menace of the redemptive mirth of rain
Is it not risible the menace?
And is it not mirthful the rain?

Rain drops stipple, they stipple the plain
They stipple the stationary window pane
Of a car without people in it.
And the faces of ordinary people,
The expressionless faces of unknown people
Standing in a shop window, looking out
Their faces hidden behind the pain

Near an old blockhouse at St. Helens
Beside the river called Columbia
Where rusty railroad ties, ruined wooden rudders,
Arrowheads and rock instruments of an aboriginal
            people,
The browning photographs of people,
Happy, sad, mirthful, depressed, long since dead
Look out from glass cases
Like people looking out from a window

The ash trees are not serious
Not serious enough
Not nearly as serious as the faces in shop windows
That an overcast sky cannot mitigate.
The reality of a shop window
And the earnestness of a late afternoon, in June,

Are nothing compared to an empty car in a parking
        lot
And the faces of unknown people

The river rolls and the river brings relief,
The river like the rain absorbs the pain,
And a seriousness with the coefficient of
        deliriousness
Fills minds cupped like hands to hold the rain

But the river does not stop,
And the mirth of the rain is not sufficient,
For the river moves, the river waves, like the rain in a
        monsoon
That moves away

Other Books by the Publisher

Fanchette's Pretty Little Foot by Restif de La Bretonne

Je M'Accuse... by Léon Bloy

My Hospitals & My Prisons by Paul Verlaine

Salvation Through the Jews by Léon Bloy

Words of a Demolitions Contractor by Léon Bloy

Cellulely by Paul Verlaine

Ecclesiastical Laurels by Jacques Rochette de la Morlière

Flowers of Bitumen by Émile Goudeau

Songs for Her & Odes in Her Honor by Paul Verlaine

On Huysmans' Tomb by Léon Bloy

Ten Years a Bohemian by Émile Goudeau

The Soul of Napoleon by Léon Bloy

Blood of the Poor by Léon Bloy

Joan of Arc and Germany by Léon Bloy

A Platonic Love by Paul Alexis

The Revealer of the Globe: Christopher Columbus & His Future Beatification (Part One) by Léon Bloy

An Immodest Proposal by Dr. Helmut Schleppend

The Pornographer by Restif de La Bretonne

Style (Theory and History) by Ernest Hello

On the Threshold of the Apocalypse: 1913-1915 by Léon Bloy

She Who Weeps (Our Lady of La Salette) by Léon Bloy

The Sylph by Claude Prosper Jolyot de Crébillon (*fils*)

Voyage in France by a Frenchman by Paul Verlaine

Curigan, Oregon by William Clark, Richard Robinson, and anonymous

Drowning by Yu Dafu

Cull of April by Francis Vielé-Griffin

The Misfortune of Monsieur Fraque by Paul Alexis

Fêtes Galantes & Songs Without Words by Paul Verlaine

Joys by Francis Vielé-Griffin

The Son of Louis XVI by Léon Bloy

Septentrion by Jean Raspail

The Resurrection of Villiers de l'Isle-Adam by Léon Bloy

Poems Saturnian by Paul Verlaine

The Biography of Léon Bloy: Memories of a Friend by René Martineau

Fredegund, France: A Book of Poetry by Richard Robinson

The Good Song by Paul Verlaine

Swans by Francis Vielé-Griffin